Venice Observed
Life in the City of Islands

By Ron Verzuh
Photos by Leola Jewett-Verzuh

Venice Observed **2**

Copyright © 2018 Ron Verzuh

Copies of this booklet can be ordered from rverzuh@shaw.ca. For more of Ron's work visit www.ronverzuh.ca.

Venice Observed 3

DEDICATION

To Calliope and Venice lovers everywhere

ACKNOWLEDGEMENTS

I thank my wife Leola Jewett-Verzuh and my daughter Alexandra Helen Verzuh, my beloved travelling companions and fellow Venice lovers. Both provided inspiration for this booklet. Leola carefully reviewed the text during the research and writing stages and made many helpful suggestions. Alex brought the endless curiosity that took us deeper and farther in our quest.

Venice Observed
Life in the City of Islands

Venice Observed **6**

She is "like many a beautiful mistress and a strong dark wine, never entirely frank with you.... Her past is enigmatic, her present contradictory, her future hazed in uncertainties."

– Jan Morris in *The World of Venice*

"This was Venice, the flattering and suspect beauty – this city, half fairy tale and half tourist trap, in whose insalubrious air the arts once rankly and voluptuously blossomed, where composers have been inspired to lulling tones of somniferous eroticism."

– Thomas Mann, author of *Death in Venice*

"Everyone's Venice is different. Where you see antiquity I see squalor. Where another marvels at beauty a second turns away in horror at some gross, naked display of poor taste. Yet it remains a place of wonder for most of us."

– David Hewson in *Carnival for the Dead*

Introducing My Venice
Welcome to La Serenissima

Why Venice? That's what some of our friends asked when we announced that we were going to spend an extended period of time "living" in the famous Italian city of canals. Why would we want to test out the 'liveability' of what they considered a damp, snobbish has-been of a city, one that was likely to disappear under the Adriatic Sea? In the essays that follow I attempt to answer that question by way of sharing some of our experiences as Venetian wannabes.

On earlier visits to Venice – I had been twice before – I was swept away by the city's magic, its magnificent art and architecture, its mystery, and its charm. I was also encouraged to purchase some colourful rubber boots in case *alta acqua* struck. That's the high water flooding that regularly visits this City of Islands, a reminder to Venetians that they are probably living on borrowed time. But the idea of living in the home city of 14th century merchant explorer Marco Polo still captivated me.

Perhaps it was the many books, fiction and non-fiction, that celebrate its greatness as well as its oddness. Tourists carrying copies of *Lonely Planet* or Rick Steves no doubt benefit from the advice within. Some may enjoy an immersion in the city through mystery writers Donna Leon, David Hewson, or Michael Didbin. But my travelling tools also included Jan Morris's *The World of Venice*, an exquisite history, travelogue, and guide to daily life all wrapped in one volume.

I had also seen Venice portrayed many times in the movies. Remember Daniel Craig's James Bond chasing down the Grand Canal in *Casino Royale* or Roger Moore as Double O7 in *Moonraker* enjoying the ritzy Hotel Danieli? Julie Christie and Donald Sutherland took us on a dark tour of the Queen of the Adriatic in *Don't Look Now*. Indiana Jones made a speedboat tour through town in *Indiana Jones and the Last Crusade*. Venice also made brief appearances in *The Talented Mister Ripley* with Matt Damon and Gwyneth Paltrow. There is the controversial Shakespearean city of *The Merchant of Venice* starring Al Pacino as Shylock. And Fellini's *Casanova*, also with Donald Sutherland, shows the great lover pursuing the objects of his desire in Venice. The list continues.

My mind set on a return visit and my head filled with these literary and Hollywood images, I wanted to get more than a tourist's view of this city so famous for its annual festival of masks, its biennale art festival, and, of course, the Venice Film Festival. Could I live in Venice? Could I make it my home for a lifetime?

Venice is a tourist magnet, to be sure, a mecca for romantics, an oasis away from cars, and a fount of beauty everywhere you look. It is also a damp, polluted cesspool, with insular and sometimes rude inhabitants, and chances are increasingly good that it will sink into the mire one day. I planned to dig deep under the touristic veneer in search of everyday life in La Serenissima, the serene place.

This group of travel essays is not meant as an exhaustive study of Venice, but rather a glimpse of some aspects of life as seen through various lenses: music, football, art, and the ubiquitous gondola. They reveal some of what I experienced at each turn in the canal, so to speak, as I try to take you beyond bustling Piazza San Marco, the heart of the city, to the nooks and crannies of this place built on water and tree stumps.

We travel to the six *sestieres* or districts, visiting the quieter corners of the city, the quarters where you find hardware stores, cheaper places to eat, and the essential wine store merchant who will fill your empty water bottle with passable *vino rosso*. We stroll through Cannaregio, where the Jewish Ghetto first got its name; Santa Croce and San Polo, with their magnificent churches, markets, and art galleries; Dorsoduro with its chichetti bars, its Accademia Bridge, and Peggy Guggenheim's collection of weird, wonderful and stark-raving modern artists; and Castello, with its Biennale Park, Arsenale naval yards, and Via Garibaldi full of cafes, bars, street markets, and art shops.

We travel on foot far from the San Marco buzz to side streets with tiny cafes, such as the delightful Osteria ai Barbacani on Calle del Paradiso (Paradise Alley), and chicetti bars like Osteria Al Squero that overlook a quiet canal. We marvel at the various watercraft, the gondolas, yes, but also the working boats that ply the waters as dump trucks, garbage collectors, bulk transporters of goods, and excavation vehicles. And we hop the city buses of Venice, the vaporetti that cruise the larger waterways at a whopping 7.50 euros per 75-minute trip.

At the end of my three weeks, I realized that living here was just a pipedream. I could no more fit into Venice than I could the North Pole. Amidst all the reasons that tempted me to stay, there was also the ever-present sense that I was a foreigner, a stranger in a magical land, forever classified a tourist. I was on a slightly longer stop than usual in one of the world's special cities, but I soon knew that I could never be a Venetian.

The essays are my way of sharing what I saw, what I liked and didn't like about one of the most enchanting cities in Europe and the world. The photographs by my wife Leola Jewett-Verzuh capture the city visually in all its colour and dramatic detail. I hope you enjoy the vicarious journey.

Venice Observed 10

Praying for the Home Team
Reflections on a Football Afternoon in Venice

First we hear it: a sub-human hum growing to an intermittent dull roar. We detect human voices uttering grunts, hoots, howls, and loud laughter. It is a low, steady, even primal shout punctuated on occasion by waves of melodic sound: "Oyeho–yeh, oyeho–yeh." The resulting buzz drowns out any vestige of the cacophony being made by the tourist crowds that jockey for a view of the Bridge of Sighs on the way to the Doge's Palace, the grand Piazza San Marco, and all the memorable sights of one of the most precious cities in Europe.

Next we see scattered groups of men of all ages, all wearing colourful scarves, some hoisting bottles of the local lager, Castello. The nearest bar has proudly hung a flag outside the entrance. It's the flag of the local football (soccer) team, Venezia F.C. Its colours are orange, green, and black. It is not a winning team, but local fans have high hopes that its purchase by a group of Americans will lift it from a third-tier team to at least a second level of competition. This Saturday they play Parma Calcio 13, a team that has known greatness but now has fallen to Venezia F.C.'s level in the standings.

Finally, we smell the gathering throng of sons and fathers, brothers, uncles, and grandfathers. The crowd comprises mostly men with the odd fearless girlfriend or wife tagging along. Everyone is sweating from the chanting and the clasping of arms in a pre-game march. Sloshing beer on each other, they are getting primed to enter the gates of the Stadio Pierluigi Penzo in the city's San Pietro neighbourhood.

We feel the tension building, the emotional temperature rising, as if some monumental event is about to unfold. The hoots and hollers of fans from all over La Serenissima, the most serene Republic of Venice, bounce off the high walls of the Arsenale naval yards from whence a once great empire's feared navy sailed. But pride in their sport and a shaky faith in their team takes priority over history. Winning today is what is important.

Some of the fans will have passed the great church of San Pietro di Castello where the waters open wide for pleasure and working boats. The most avid fans will have perhaps kneeled in one of the districts 14 churches to say a prayer for the team. Perhaps they did so at La Pieta Church, where composer Antonio Vivaldi once preached. It sits somberly just a few blocks down the Revi degli Schiavoni, the long stretch of waterfront with its pricey hotels and equally pricey restaurants.

Further north at Fondamente Nove, a main stop for vaporetti, Venice's water buses, fans pour onto the dock where flocks of tourists await the next vaporetto en route to the glassblowing island of Murano and the lace-making island of Burano. The football fans arriving from these smaller islands will have passed the cemetery island of San Michelle on their way to the game. Perhaps a quiet prayer is said as they pass the graves of the American poet Ezra Pound or composer Igor Stravinsky, who are among the many famous Venetians and expats buried there. The vaporetto also passes two of the world's great poets, Dante and Virgil, as they are rowed to purgatory. Alas, neither was known for his love of football.

The fans clutch their coveted team scarves as they cluster at the turnstile while husky ticket checkers wearing New York Yankees baseball caps slow their progress. This is not a crowd that will accept any long delays due to bureaucracy. They will cheer on their heroes today just as the public cheered the classical heroes of another age immortalized in stone in nearby

Biennale Park. This Saturday, the grand art festival, the Biennale, uses the park for its exhibits from around the world, but it is of little interest to the fans.

At lunch earlier, some of them had streamed past the sidewalk cafes, used clothing stores, outdoor markets, and gelato shops along Via Garibaldi, a pedestrian boulevard named after one of the heroes of the Risorgimento, Italy's 19th-century unification movement. I noticed the men passing, their scarves matching the bright orange of my Spritz, the locally popular prosecco and aperal cocktail.

Unflustered by the gathering football mob, a young accordion player places a stool on the paving stones nearby and sets out his plastic bowl for donations. He begins his serenade of the passersby with a rendition of the Beatles' *Let It Be*, then shows off his finger work on *O Sole Mio*. Farther down the wide street, fans can be heard chanting as if they are part of some medieval monks' pilgrimage. This is soon drowned out by the voices of many singers issuing from a cafe. It is a wonderfully invigorating sound from a group of opera-singing Pied Pipers that draws street traffic to the entrance in hopes of sharing their moment of joy. The patrons and kitchen staff alike join arms in singing a song of victory that the footballers cheer as they pass.

At the bar next door, four middle-aged men lounge in the sun, beer mugs in hand, waiting for the crowds to dissipate before rushing off to the stadium gates. The chubbiest of the foursome is balding more than the others. He wears a T-shirt that says "Let's Hug It Out!" That suggests he is not in quite the fighting spirit required to beat Parma today, but perhaps it is more in keeping with the modern Venetian style.

If one reads the growing collection of America author Donna Leon's Commissario Brunetti murder mysteries, the Veneto is filled with graft, corruption, and bloody murder. But a stroll into the side streets of Dorsoduro, Cannaregio, and most certainly the sestiere (district) of Castello, where the football stadium is situated, suggest a sleepy city not so troubled by crime.

Here, as elsewhere, the quiet is broken only by a motorized launch rounding a canal corner or a hand porter yelling "Attenzione, attenzione." The latter are as agile as football players when it comes to negotiating their way around the mass of tourists.

This ancient place is flush with riches transported to it by merchants like Marco Polo or plundered by the doge's marauding armies of the Crusades. This may be a deeply Catholic town, but Mammon ruled in those days. Venice's armies even sacked Constantinople, a fellow Christian city, and sailed home with the looted silver and gold.

Galleries such as the Accademia are plump with medieval and Renaissance art that depicts the empire's great battles alongside notable Biblical events. Titian, Tintoretto, Tiepolo, the Bellinis, Veronese, Carpaccio, are among the world-class artists that left works behind to adorn their city. Paintings of Christ on the cross dominate.

Peggy Guggenheim also brought a wealth of art to the city, but it probably was not the kind that many footballers and their fans would appreciate. Among the Picassos, Modiglianis, Chagalls, Pollocks, and Dalis, there might be found exceptions to that rule. They would no doubt guffaw on seeing Marino Marini's equestrian statue on the Guggenheim terrace. He is in full penis erectus as he gallops forth never to reach the Grand Canal. It has a distinct locker-room quality about it.

Alas, footballers' prayers, chants, and opera arias have done no good. Venezia F.C. lost to Parma, 1-0, that Saturday. The team will survive to play other games, its fans following it to the end. And so it is with Venice itself. Its fans will always love it. They will complain about the tourists, about the threatening high water, the high prices, and the slow sinking of their island home. They will continue to confess their sins at churches all over the city's six districts, including the synagogues of Cannaregio near Santa Lucia train station.

Jan Morris, who is among the best modern travel writers anywhere, describes Venice in a way that a Venetia F.C. team member might understand. She is "like many a beautiful mistress and a strong dark wine, never entirely frank with you," writes Morris. "Her past is enigmatic, her present contradictory, her future hazed in uncertainties." It is thus with football in the Serenissima these days.

Venice Observed 16

Gondola, Gondola

In Venice where black ghost ships carry lovers of all ages

Everywhere in Venice, you will find gondolas. This is no secret. It is after all, a city of water streets crammed with these sleek black ghost ships lurking about day and night in search of human cargo. They are lined up side by side at the quay closest to the Piazza San Marco. More of them bob and duck near the busy Zaccaria vaporetto station and from the top of Rialto Bridge or Accademia Bridge one sees them plying their way up and down the Grand Canal trolling for lovers.

Even the narrowest waterways in this canal-divided city will find themselves invaded by a gondolier singing *O Sole Mio* or some other standard tune that is believed to please the tourist willing to pay 100 euros for the pleasure of stepping aboard. Often an accordionist supplies the musical accompaniment thus further enticing lovers old and young, Asian and Caucasian, African and North American, to feel the air transformed by magic love dust once they are on board one of the hundreds of black, flat-bottomed vessels.

There are alternatives to the expensive rides the gondoliers, punching at their cellphones to kill time, will coax you to buy. You can share with others, of course, splitting the cost. The downside: Your photos will include the faces of total strangers. You might also get a seat facing the gondolier and every shot you take will have him in it. But hey, if you want the cheap seats, you have to pay.

The great lover Casonova lived here long ago and used a gondola to seek out his latest amorous conquest. The greatest of Venetian artists, Titian, rode to his latest masterpiece in a hooded gondola. Vivaldi, the city's famed composer, too, would hop aboard one of the shiny wooden steeds to be delivered to his sermon as the priest of La Pieta Church on the Reva degli Schiavoni. The doge, once Venice's chief ruler, had his own special gondola with its own garage.

Gondolas are the black princes of the city's vast network of waterways, a large-scale Snakes and Ladders mapscape. And their oarsmen are skilled at appealing to the tourist trade. Their uniform of red-striped shirts and straw-boater-style hats can be seen at various bridges where the crafts are gathered three across waiting for another couple to be seated in the gold-trimmed, red-cushioned bench with their cameras at the ready.

Gondolas are said to have originated as ancient rowboats more than 1,000 years ago. Over the centuries they evolved, but 15th-century paintings by Carpaccio and one of the Bellinis show them to be similar to the ones we see today. The arrival of the steam engine in the 19th century bumped them out of the running for most efficient transport.

They were forced to the edge of Venice's water routes by engine-driven boats of all kinds. Car ferries pass by San Marco Basin on their way to the sunbathing island of Lido, where cars are allowed. Massive sailing cities block the view of San Giorgio Maggiore church across from Piazza San Marco as tugs push and pull them to dock at Tronchetto where they will disgorge their passengers wide-eyed with wonder.

Today, these richly ornamented vessels are reserved for the transporting of dreamers lost in the romance of the miraculous Byzantine San Marco basilica, and in the mystery and history of forgotten empire. Venetians take pride in the handsome if disorganized fleet, but few will pay the price of a gondola these days.

The cheapest way to experience a gondola ride is by taking a short jaunt across the Grand Canal in what is called a traghetto. This is a no frills gondola that for two euro will take you to the other side. For another two they will take you back where you came from. But it is hardly a true representation of what you get if you actually dig deep into your tourist budget to step into the real thing.

Gondolas are magical vessels akin to limousines. The traghetto is a yellow cab. One is for pleasure, the other for convenience. The yellow cab will always look in need of care while the limousine enjoys the benefit of having a gondola repair shop on the Trovaso River not far from the Accademia Bridge. Looking at the shop from the top of a beer glass at the chichetti bar Osteria Al Squero, it resembles a graveyard for small whales more than a place of restoration. The dark hulks lay on their sides awaiting the skilled craftsmen who will make them canal worthy and therefore tourist worthy again.

Watching them navigate among Venice's watery crevasses, majestic in an awkward sort of way, it is strange to see these idle, incapacitated, inanimate carcasses perhaps revealing a decaying side of the once glamourous Serenissima. But no! These bodies – about 400 of them are active, down from 10,000 a few centuries ago – will be revived and restored to their former glory. They will again sneer at the lesser traghetto trundling back and forth.

Is gondola making an art or a craft? The men in a woodworking workshop not far from Peggy Guggenheim's collection of weird and wonderful paintings and sculptures would probably argue that they are artists. If you can find them in the twisting streets of the Dorsoduro district with its trinket stores, wine shops, and dead end streets, you will see these worker-artists meticulously carving the oarlocks or forcolas essential to the smooth operation of a gondola.

Certainly, gondolas influenced the creative minds that shaped Venice on the huge canvasses displayed at the Accademia, Ca' Rezzonica, or Punta Della Dogana Museum near the magnificent La Salute Church and all the dozens of churches that house and protect these treasures of earlier times. They are often in the foreground of giant images telling the history of the city and its inhabitants from century to century.

If gondolas are not an art form, they inspire art. They also inspired the owner of the Alta Acqua bookstore, the most unique in Venice or almost anywhere else, to place an expired gondola in the middle of his shop and fill it with enough books to sink it. They also inspire various forms of kitch art as the many vending carts selling gondola ornaments along the Reva degli Schiavoni will attest.

For the wealthier visitor, a gondola made of blown glass in the factories of Murano where gondolas also ferry tourists along its canals, would be an extravagant mantelpiece. For most of us, though, a trinket will serve nicely as a momento with which to celebrate the beauty of this distinctive and enduringly captivating water vehicle.

Musical Conundrum in the Veneto
From *La Traviata*, to *O Sole Mio* and *That's Amore*

My wife hates *That's Amore*. She just can't get her head around the moon being likened to a big pizza pie, so it was with apprehension that she made her shopping excursions into the Venetian tourist tumult on the bustling Rialto Bridge. She went armed with a set of earplugs in the certainty that *That's Amore* would ripple from the numerous jewelry stores, Murano glass shops, stationery specialists, and even some market stalls.

Later that day, she was able to further distance herself from Deano Martin, the pizza pie moon man, when she learned that she could attend an opera at La Fenice, one of the most famous opera houses in the world. After a dinner of Pasta-To-Go spaghetti, part of Venice's growing fast food industry, we wandered past old San Moise church where ordinary San Marco Venetians worship, leaving the nearby basilica to the tourists.

La Fenice is just a block away and awaiting us was *La Traviata*, the Giuseppe Verdi opera. Soon enough the grand hall was ablaze with the banished love of Alfredo and Violetta. Ablaze is a bad choice of words given that the building, erected in the 1770s, burnt down in 1996. But it is now lovingly restored to its former grandeur.

When we visited the theatre earlier, having read about its death and resurrection (fenice is phoenix in Italian) in journalist John Berendt's *The City of Falling Angels,* we were advised that just to see the theatre would cost us 10 euro. The cheapest seats cost 25 euro for the pleasure of sitting in the rafters. I was reluctant but my wife added a further inducement: she offered to pay.

Hearing the offer in one ear, out of the other I overheard a Scottish couple discussing the plot of the opera. "Is it really worth it?" a Scottish woman asked. "Well, dearie," said her husband, "it's like all operas I've ever seen: Violetta dies, Alfredo is heartbroken, and his father is ashamed for keeping the two apart to preserve the family's honour." No matter. We were about to enjoy a fine evening at a world-class theatre, comparable to Lincoln Center in New York, The Bolshoi Theatre in Moscow, or the Sydney Opera House.

I was filled with anticipation as we walked up five flights of stairs to reach the low-ceilinged top tier of the building. Getting a drink during the intermission was going to mean a good 10-minute walk, but I put that minor inconvenience aside. After all, we were going to see an opera at La Fenice. Then my heart sank.

As soon as the opera began, an elderly German woman who was sitting in the front row of our section decided to lean close to the railing blocking my view of the stage. I wished away any malice; she would soon lean back and enjoy the show. But no, I was only able to see the performance through her hair. I thought of those Disney cartoons where a man with an Afro or wearing a top hat sits in front of Bugs Bunny or Yosemite Sam. What to do?

Sam would have blown her away with his six shooters, but I did not have that option. I considered pushing her over the edge at intermission or the less Draconian measure of asking her politely to lean back. Perhaps I could remove myself to a standing position in the aisle. Option one was obviously out of the question, death is a common occurrence in most operas, but the cost would be prohibitive. The second option might have worked, but I speak no German and my wife, reading my mind, frowned at my suggestion. Standing in the aisle was also a nonstarter. The ushers patrol those areas regularly and abide by a simple rule: no seat, no show. As a small consolation for my viewing sacrifice, I did manage to sneak a teensy peek at Violetta dying.

Thankfully, my musical experiences in Venice were not all so troubling. For example, we were always able to enjoy the five-piece ensembles that play, rain or shine, in Piazza San Marco. Always crowded with pigeons, tourists, trinket sellers, photographers, and newly weds, it makes for a bizarre dance floor. Lurking pickpockets in this tiny perfect city find their game among the dancers and music lovers forever congregating in the piazza.

Warning note: the ensembles are there for the enjoyment of guests who choose to drop double-digit amounts of euro for the pleasure of sipping caffè lattes. It is rather pleasing music and the temptation is strong to sit down at one of the linen-clothed tables in front of, say, the Florian, the most famous and priciest of San Marco cafes. A waiter will quickly remove you with a snooty attitude that I thought was reserved for his Parisian counterparts.

As with my Fenice experience, there were options. One, I could refuse to leave the table, risking a stay in a Venetian jail, perhaps transported shackled across the Bridge of Spies never to see Venice again. Two, I could produce a protest sign, claiming that my human rights were being violated. That might get me beat up by music-loving onlookers. The third option was to buy a double-scoop of gelato ice cream next door – nocciola is my favourite flavour. We took that option with delicious pleasure and sat on the cold marble steps of the piazza's periphery. From there, I occasionally thumbed my nose at the nasty waiter.

The bands, usually with piano, trumpet, violin, clarinet, and base, all together now, induced in us a desire to dance. We fought off the desire, but other couples began to waltz amidst the splatting sound of blue and red plastic blobs that men of unknown origin were tossing on the piazza tiles in a losing attempt to entice people to buy the gelatinous substance.

Inevitably, the dancers shuffling through the mob would bump into another vendor, possibly an Ethiopian perhaps taking final revenge for Mussolini's invasion of his country. This one is selling red roses. Nay, not selling, but rather pressing them into the male dancer's chest and looking up at him with begging eyes. Heaven knows how he supports his family in his line of work, but Venice makes a place for him and so many others seeking to survive on tourist euros.

Strolling down the Reva degli Schiavoni, we encounter cafe violinists and accordionists near the Bridge of Sighs. Farther down we meet with other special musical experiences. There is the young man on Via Garibaldi punching out various standards on his concertina. I am tempted to warn him not to play *That's Amore*, but am too late. The young man, perhaps sensing danger, switches to *Let It Be*, but my wife is unwilling.

Our musical adventures culminated at La Pieta Church on the Reva. Covered in construction awnings and curtains, it is impossible to see the structure that is usually pictured in the guidebooks. Inside, however, we learn that this is composer Antonio Vivaldi's home church. In fact, they say he preached here and was known as the Red Priest on account of his red hair.

It might be apocryphal, but who cares? We are in luck. There is a concert in the church that evening. A harpsichord, three violins, a viola, a cello, and a base will give a rendition of Vivaldi's *Four Seasons*. The lead violinist plays his heart out for us surrounded by the disturbing faceless images of Bosnian artist Safet Zec. The music seems incongruous with Zec's black and white bodies entwined in agony. Are the hands and arms wrapped protectively around the body of Christ, or are they representations of the brutality and suffering that mark historic events in his birth country?

Artist and violin virtuoso are akin to rock stars for my wife. She is in ecstasy. Not quite the Rolling Stones or Michelangelo, I think, but it is a sterling performance rousing the audience to a prolonged standing ovation.

Outside on the rain-drenched Reva, I rush my wife under a too-small umbrella as we start back to the piazza. On the way, I hear the distinctive strains of a lone cellist, playing what sounds like, you guess it, *That's Amore*.

Venice Observed 26

Lasting Impressions of Venice
The good, the not so good, and the outrageous

In a chicetti bar on the River Trovaso

I'm sitting on a hard wooden bench in a chicetti bar on the Trovaso River, a wide canal that juts off the lengthy Guidecca Canal walkway called the Zattere. Exactly opposite several workers busy themselves at a gondola repair shop in the Dorsoduro district of Venice. It's 4:30 p.m. and the sun is brightly gleaming into the Osteria Al Squero, Venice's version of a tapas bar.

Multilingual voices emanate from the bar to the quay, or *fondamente*, and other voices seem to bounce back. Lovers' quarrels mingle with artists' consultations about the best angle to choose in oil or water-colour renderings of the chapel of San Trovasio. At that moment, one of the city's green garbage boats squeezes between three other parked boats. Hardly the picture-perfect scene the artists want, but nonetheless an integral part of life in Venice.

Across from me in the bar, an elderly man and woman sip Bellinis and mutter in French about Venice being too crowded now, then switch topics to what to eat for dinner; she wants fish, he wants pasta. Bets are he will win or that they will compromise on a thin-crusted anchovy and mushroom pizza. The resolution is drowned out by the engines of two water taxis. These are a mode of transport that only the rich or the willfully extravagant can afford. The slight scent of petrol seeps up from the canal as they motor past just missing a collision with the garbage boat.

Nearby, two young men are sharing an electric cigarette as both bend over their cellphones. They could be twins or gay lovers. Their matching white hair shines in the sunlight. They have their Bellinis balanced on the quay railing but in plastic cups that dull the bright red-orange colour. Soon they are joined by a gaggle of thirsty German tourists who crowd the chicetti bar and order beer *alla spina* (draft) and munch the tiny seafood sandwiches among other delicacies placed enticingly before them.

    In an hour or so, they will climb into a *vaporetto* (water bus) and be shuttled back to their cruise ship for dinner or to a hotel in nearby Mestre to prep for an evening at the Goldoni Theatre or at a church performance (costumed or not) of Antonio Vivaldi's *Four Seasons*. They may also opt for a stroll along the Zattere to its tip marked by the spectacular La Salute Church with its stunning blue mermaid sculpture.

    They are members of the great mass of tourists who will add steadily to the work of the green-uniformed garbage workers, especially the large gatherings in Piazza San Marco. There they join the circus of humanity, pigeons, photographers, sketch artists, and small yappy dogs that merge in front of the Byzantine Basilica San Marco, the 100-metre tall Campanile tower, and the unique clock tower that sits catty corner to the basilica.

    Here lovers pose, one holding a selfie stick, the other clowning for the camera. Strangers stroll by, rejecting the prods of rose sellers and trinket vendors. Children chase pigeons. Little boys try fruitlessly to kick the birds, but the ubiquitous birds are aware of the danger and almost always manage to flutter past it. A boy slips and is scolded by his parents.

    As the sky darkens, men of uncertain origin flip tiny, lighted objects high into the air in hopes of a sale, but no one buys. No one quite knows what the objects are. Other men splat plastic on the paving stones. Again, though, it is a puzzling and pointless act for no one except the odd pestered parent would bother to placate a child by purchasing the useless substance. I am reminded of the pet rock craze that captivated the gullible public some decades ago.

Couples waltz to the chamber music spreading from one too-expensive outdoor cafe to another. The rose pushers and splatters are also dancing after a fashion. They flit from one multilingual group of tourists to another, flogging their wares and pressing cheap plastic into the unsuspecting hands of strollers who almost invariably reject the offer. Their dance is one of survival rather than pleasure. And yet they appear better off than the old lady dressed all in black who crouches in the piazza, her scarfed head covering her shame, her plastic cup extended.

At lunch earlier, a young couple from Atlanta, Georgia, breathlessly described how dazzled they were by what some call the Queen of the Adriatic or The City of Masks. They have just arrived a mere month after becoming engaged. He is Jewish, an accountant. She will convert, she says, making his parents happy and more agreeable. But for her parents, they might have eloped to this wedding-crazy city.

On almost any morning, the couple might be inspired by a fresh pair of newly weds – she shivering in white strapless gown and he in black tux – posing with San Giorgio Maggiore church in the background. Occasionally, the photographer must wait while two or three tugs slowly guide a giant ocean liner through San Marco Basin to dock at Piazzale Roma and Torchetto.

Alas, the Georgia couple has passed on the elopement idea, romantic as it might have seemed. They won't have time for the dancing either. Nor will they sample the prosecco at the Osteria Al Squero. Like so many three-day visitors, they will try to see everything this magical city offers. But they will leave not knowing that they have failed.

In Venice's Jewish Ghetto

There are very few Jews living in the sestiere (district) of Cannaregio now, but there was a time before the Holocaust when they formed a community and could worship at as many as five synagogues. They lived safely in this comfortable neighbourhood with its less busy canals, inexpensive cafes, and flourishing bar scene. We had hoped to spend time at the ghetto museum learning more about that community and what happened to it, but our plans were frustrated by an incident that dulled our interest.

We had been to the Campo del Ghetto before and were getting used to flitting from one fondamente (quayside) to another, weaving to and fro through narrow dead-end streets, being caught in wrong turns, and then backtracking as is customary all over Venice. This time we beat the map and walked straight to the campo from Guglie Bridge a block north of the Grand Canal. The crowds dissipated as we moved farther away from the thoroughfare that carries foot traffic into the city's centre from Santa Lucia train station.

Soon we were enjoying the relative tranquility of the campo. We ate a kosher lunch across the square from the museum, snapped a photo of a Hasidic man playing with his son, viewed several sculptured panels depicting the horrors of the Holocaust, and stepped up to the museum entrance. A goateed young man blocked our entry and told us to empty our pockets and put our bags on a conveyer belt similar to what we would do at an airport.

At this point, I was getting flustered. Why all the fuss over security? It's a museum, not a military installation. The sombre young man saw that I was irritated and made me even more so by patting me down with a metal-detecting wand. I retrieved my bag, giving him my most disgusted look.

"Is it the current Israeli government that ordered such a rigorous search of museum visitors," I asked, me with the big chip on my shoulder, as I stepped away to enter the museum. Suddenly, he stopped me: "Do you have a knife in your pocket?" That was it. I turned and walked away angry at being subjected to the indignity of a search. Upon reflection I wondered if it was the museum curator's way of giving us this added personal experience of what it is like to be demeaned? If so, he succeeded.

Bull in a Murano glass shop

Like thousands of other visitors to Venice, we spent a lot of our time shopping for glass. And glass was enticingly and extravagantly displayed everywhere with signage boasting that it was from the famous glass-blowing island of Murano.

Fortified with warnings from Murano glass factory guides about cheap Chinese imitations, we wandered into a Piazza San Marco shop in search of a kitchen lamp. I'm tall so was wary of bumping one of the delicate glass pieces. Alas, no precaution short of me staying outside the shop would have prevented disaster.

"Look at this one, dear," my wife called from the other side of the shop. I turned to look and smashed my forehead into a beautiful crystal chandelier. The next thing I heard was the tinkle of glass falling to the floor and breaking into hundreds of tiny pieces. "Could that have been me?" I said astonished. By then the shop clerk, a small middle-aged woman, was sweeping up the damage. "What do we do?" I asked her. She did not seem to understand, but swooping in behind me was a man who appeared to be in charge.

I asked the same question of him, but he was already on his cellphone apparently seeking the answer. When he hung up, I asked a third time but got no joy from his response. "Well, it is 150 euro of damage," he said, and I recalled at that instant seeing the price tag on the fixture. It was 2,400 euro. "But I cannot ask you to pay so much," the man added with a sorrowful look. I later learned that his name was Stefano and that he worked for a cooperative comprising four such shops in the piazza.

"Let us say 50 euro," he offered almost as if he was doing us a favour. I reached for my credit card but my wife stopped me. Did she sense that something was amiss? She had snapped a photo of a part of the breakage that was sitting loosely in the chandelier. Was this a setup? The man had quickly grabbed it when he entered. "We'll pay you in cash," she said, adding with great presence of mind, "and we want a receipt."

I felt strange about the whole affair and had pressed Stefano. "Surely others have smacked into the low-hanging fixtures." Apparently not. "Never in my 30 years here has anyone ever done so, signor." I didn't believe a word of it, but we were stuck. A day before our departure, with zero alternatives to handing him 50 euro, we succumbed.

Later, I kicked myself for not calling the carabinieri. The local police could easily have sorted it out. At the very least the threat of calling the police might have exposed Stefano's scam. Then again, after 30 years maybe the police and he have an 'arrangement'?

As we left the shop and walked disconsolately through the piazza my wife offered me solace. The next day we found the light fixture we wanted and for an acceptable price including insurance and shipping. It now hangs in our kitchen as a daily reminder.

Alphonso the dachshund and other dogs

Venice, as elsewhere in Italy, is doggy heaven. Take Alphonso the dachshund. He's a happy little fellow, tripping along a *rio tera* (reclaimed street) or slipping through a *sotoportego* (covered passageway) his master or mistress fumbling with his leash and juggling the morning's shopping purchases from the local coop.

Alphonso has many friends. There is the mini-boxer Casanova who often suns himself spread-eagle on Strada Nova, the main thoroughfare leading to Piazza San Marco. Fifi, the poodle-pug cross, also circulates regularly in the neighbourhood doing her business with great regularity.

Wander down any narrow street and you are soon confronted with Alphonso and company. Amazingly, the streets tend to be clear of doggie doo. Rarely is there a Stoop and Scoop sign to remind dog owners of their civic duty. In a place as compact as Venice, garbage removal and recycling are priorities. Tourism being the major revenue generator means that merchants will insist on clean streets.

Hired dog walkers can be seen with as many as five or six dogs on separate leashes crisscrossing through various piazzas. Some of these hirelings have no interest in their charges and they show no affection for them. Others are aware that they have been entrusted with a precious family member. If a nasty child tries to kick at a Venetian dog, they risk having the walker kick back.

As I observed the comings and goings of Venetian dogs, I wondered how our dog Poppy would fit in with Alphonso, Fifi, and Casanova. Then I recalled that she is afraid of water.

Venice Observed **34**

Arrivederci Venice
Goodbye, oh "flattering and suspect beauty"

As we wound our way up the Grand Canal on the vaporetto for a final tour, Venice in its splendour and gaudiness popped out at us from all sides. There was the naked horseman on Peggy Guggenheim's terrace. Two huge white hands emerged out of the dark waters, announcing the Biennale arts festival. Lovers attached their locks to the Accademia Bridge as we passed under it. A beggar in black bowed her scarf-covered head near the canal's edge, hoping for whatever the tourists would spare. A block north on the Strada Nova, a sidewalk artist chalked another Primavera in pastels for passersby. They stop to gawk, possibly toss a coin, then hustle off to join the endless stream of humans, dogs, cats, and vendors' carts.

Travelling the canal is a sightseer's delight, a city bus tour on water that lets you see memorable sights that are otherwise inaccessible. The vaporetto does all the work. There are no narrow dead-end streets to worry about. No sotoportegos that lead only to a watery *cul de sac*.

On board, passengers bump and grind to the rhythm of these workhorses, hear the chug of the engine, and feel the thump of a rough landing at the floating yellow-striped stations. They hear a multitude of languages spoken, experience the wind blowing in their hair, and are amazed to see a Venetian woman unperturbed by the rock and roll of the boat as she reads her morning *Il Gazzetino*.

All around us, the water bubbles with water traffic. The black gondolas fight the waves made by the sleek water taxis. Tugs push giant floating cities to their docks at Tronchetto. Traghettos wait for their chance to slip across the canal between vaporetti ferrying tourists to the other side of the wide canal at two euro a crossing. Working craft go about the business of keeping the city functioning if not always flourishing.

We pass under the Rialto Bridge, most famous of all four canal spans. Shoppers rush to the fish market nearby while tourists search the tiny shops on either side of the bridge in search of a piece of oh-so-special Murano glass or delicate Burano lace. Others hunt for the best deal on fresh produce in the nearby vegetable market only to find that prices vary little if at all. Soon we are under the Scalzi Bridge, steering travellers, arms laden with suitcases, to Santa Lucia train station where they will say farewell. Others cross on the newest of the bridges, the modern, curvy Calatrava Bridge.

Arriving by train, the visitor follows the crowds from all over Italy to exit into the spectacle that awaits them. Stepping from the station, the dome of San Simeone Piccolo smiles at you and then you are hit by the rush of boat and pedestrian traffic frantically moving up and down the Grand Canal. On the crowded Lista di Spagna you walk into the world of Venice, into a fabulous world of art, architecture, history, gastronomy, football, and Vivaldi.

Now, as we contemplate our departure, we know this could never be home. But it will never be far from our minds either. This City of Masks has won our hearts and at once captivated and frustrated us. Arrivederci, I say, to a place novelist Thomas Mann once called a "flattering and suspect beauty." We will return some day, but until then I hope that a great *alta acqua* does not engulf this city of dreams.

IMAGES

Page 1 – Gondoliers on the Grand Canal
Page 2 – Arch upon arch
Page 3 – San Marco Basilica
Page 4 – Accademia Bridge (top) and Rialto Bridge
Page 5 – The Bridge of Sighs
Page 6 – One of many Venetian doorknockers
Page 10 – La Fenice Opera House and Vivaldi
Page 15 – Lone gondolier in search of a canal, vaporetti
Page 16 – Texting gondolier, traghetto landing
Page 20 – Alta Acqua bookstore
Page 25 – Classy gondola, canine gondola rider
Page 26 – Ghetto visitors google, Holocaust sculpture
Page 34 – Gondola repair yards, woman in chicetti bar
Page 37 – Punta Della Dogana Museum, Dante & Virgil
Page 38 – The author at the Accademia Gallery
Page 39 – Fido rests, Osteria ai Barbacani
Page 40 – Pavement Primavera

ABOUT THE AUTHOR

Ron Verzuh is a Canadian writer, historian, photographer, and documentary filmmaker with a life-long love of travel. He is married and has one daughter, two stepdaughters, five step granddaughters, and a great granddaughter named Calliope. May she see the world and learn from it.

Photo by Leola Jewett-Verzuh taken at the Accademia Gallery, Venice. Painting is Gentile Bellini's Miracle of the Cross at the Bridge of San Lorenzo, *circa 1500.*

Venice Observed **39**

TRAVELLER'S NOTES

_____
_____
_____
_____
_____
_____
_____
_____

TRAVELLER'S NOTES

_____
_____
_____
_____
_____
_____
_____
_____
_____
_____

Made in the USA
Lexington, KY
17 December 2017